Voices of the AMERICAN REVOLUTION
STORIES FROM THE BATTLEFIELDS

by Lois Miner Huey

Consultant:
Robert Allison, PhD
Professor of History
Chair, History Department
Suffolk University
Boston, Massachusetts

CAPSTONE PRESS
a capstone imprint

Edge Books are published by Capstone Press,
1710 Roe Crest Drive, North Mankato, Minnesota 56003.
www.capstonepub.com

 Books published by Capstone Press are manufactured with paper
containing at least 10 percent post-consumer waste.

Library of Congress Cataloging-in-Publication Data
Huey, Lois Miner.
  Voices of the American Revolution : stories from the battlefields / by
    Lois Miner Huey.
      p. cm.— (Edge books. Voices of war)
  Includes bibliographical references and index.
  ISBN: 978-1-4296-4739-7 (library binding)
  ISBN: 978-1-4296-5628-3 (paperback)
  1. United States—History—Revolution, 1775–1783—Biography—
    Juvenile literature. I. Title. II. Series.
  E302.5.H83 2011
  973.3092'2—dc22   2010000997

Editorial Credits

Kathryn Clay, editor; Tracy Davies, designer; Svetlana Zhurkin,
    media researcher; Laura Manthe, production specialist

Photo Credits

Architect of the Capitol, 28; The Bridgeman Art Library/American Illustrators Gallery,
New York, 18; Getty Images/Hulton Archive, 24; Getty Images/Kean Collection, 10;
Getty Images/MPI, 7; Getty Images National Geographic/Louis S. Glanzman, 23;
Getty Images/Popperfoto, 17; The Granger Collection, New York, 9; Library of
Congress, cover (letter), 25; Line of Battle Enterprise, cover (top); Mary Evans Picture
Library, 15; North Wind Picture Archives, 6, 11, 12, 14, 19, 21, 22, 26–27; Shutterstock/
Adam Tinney (flames), cover, back cover, 1; Shutterstock/Ann Triling (stars),
throughout; Shutterstock/argus (flag), cover; Shutterstock/Cagri Oner (torn paper),
throughout; Shutterstock/egd (drummer), cover; Shutterstock/Igorsky (stone wall), 9,
13, 21, 25; Shutterstock/kzww (rusty background), throughout; Shutterstock/Lora Liu
(paper background), throughout; Shutterstock/Sergey Kamshylin (smoke), cover, back
cover, 1; Wikimedia, 26 (top); XNR Productions (map), 5

Printed in the United States of America in North Mankato, Minnesota.
032013   007240R

TABLE OF CONTENTS

1 THE START OF A REVOLUTION

In the late 1700s, 13 **colonies** in North America stretched along the Atlantic coast. They were ruled and protected by Great Britain for more than 100 years. But then Britain began passing new laws. The British demanded that Americans pay more taxes. Some Americans wanted to fight for freedom from these rules. They called themselves patriots. The British called them rebels.

Patriots from each colony met to discuss the new taxes. Thinking war was near, some practiced marching and shooting firearms. Others showed their anger by throwing crates of tea into the Boston Harbor in December 1773. This event became known as the Boston Tea Party.

In April 1775, British soldiers marched out of Boston, Massachusetts. They planned to capture firearms from the American colonists. But the colonists learned that the British were coming. They were ready to fight back.

At first, the American army, or Continental army, could not win any battles. The British had the best army in the world. Over time, the Americans began to win small battles. Then they won major battles. In 1783, the Americans won the war with help from France.

People from both sides had unforgettable stories to tell after the war. You're about to learn the details of a few of them.

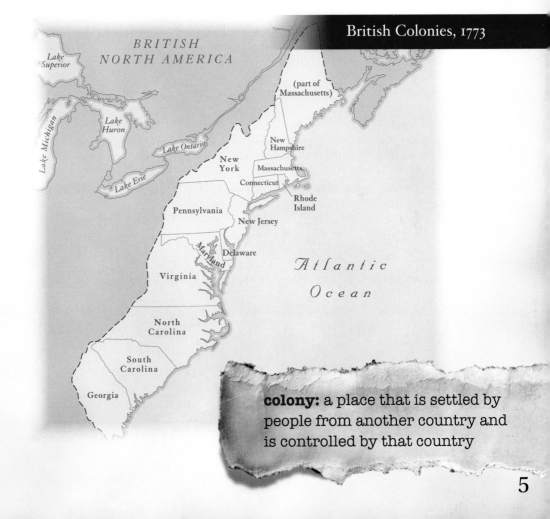

British Colonies, 1773

BRITISH NORTH AMERICA

Lake Superior

Lake Michigan

Lake Huron

Lake Ontario

Lake Erie

(part of Massachusetts)

New Hampshire

New York

Massachusetts

Connecticut

Rhode Island

Pennsylvania

New Jersey

Delaware

Maryland

Virginia

North Carolina

South Carolina

Georgia

Atlantic Ocean

colony: a place that is settled by people from another country and is controlled by that country

5

2 ANDREW SHERBURNE: AMERICAN SAILOR

recruiting privateers

Like many boys in the 1700s, 13-year-old Andrew Sherburne dreamed of being a sailor. His parents agreed to let him join his uncles and 30 other boys aboard the warship *Ranger* in June 1779. The boys helped the American sailors by coiling rope, repairing sails, stocking supplies, and cooking. Eventually they would learn to be sailors too.

Sherburne's job was to stack gunpowder and cannonballs by the guns. In his first battle against the British, Sherburne was surrounded by gun blasts, smoke, and shouting men. His chest tightened with fear, but he managed to complete his duties. When a 24-pound (11-kilogram) cannonball slammed into the ship's side, Sherburne quickly jumped back. The ball just missed him.

The crew aboard the *Ranger* lost the battle and was captured by the British. The British traded a wounded American officer for a British officer who had been captured earlier. Sherburne was released so he could help take the injured soldier home. He was happy to be released, but he knew he wasn't finished fighting. Once home, Sherburne rejoined the war. He served on two other navy ships before signing onto a **privateer** in April 1781.

Americans fighting aboard the USS *Alliance*

privateer: a private ship that is authorized to attack enemy ships during wartime; the sailors aboard are also called privateers

CAPTURED AGAIN

Aboard the privateer, Sherburne helped work the sails. He also raided enemy ships. After several months, the British captured the privateer during a brief fight. But Sherburne wasn't released this time. In January 1782, he was thrown into a British prison.

Other American prisoners learned Sherburne had only six months of schooling. They taught him writing and math. But within a few months, Sherburne became very ill. A raging fever made him act strangely, so he had to be watched closely. He also suffered from aching muscles, chills, and vomiting.

Eventually Sherburne and others were traded for British prisoners. When Sherburne left prison, he was still very weak. He could walk to the ship only with the help of two canes.

Back in the colonies, Sherburne recovered and joined another ship. Soon after, he was captured a third time. This time he suffered from hunger and sickness aboard a dirty prison ship. Sherburne was 18 years old and in poor health when the war ended in 1783. His sailing days were over. But thanks to his prison education, he became a successful surveyor and schoolteacher.

Conditions were miserable aboard British prison ships.

Aboard the Prison Ships

During the war, British soldiers occupied New York City. They kept anchored ships in nearby harbors to use as prisons for American captives. Prisoners slept shoulder-to-shoulder in the crowded ships. They received little food and were covered with fleas and lice. Rats scurried around them. Some prisoners didn't have any clothes. Because of these poor conditions, many prisoners died each day. Of the 25,000 Americans who died during the war, more than 11,000 died aboard prison ships.

3 JULIUS WASMUS: GERMAN DOCTOR

helping an injured soldier

Dr. Julius Wasmus watched as horses were being lifted onto a ship. Wasmus was joining other Germans hired to help the British fight the Americans. As Wasmus sailed toward the colonies, he didn't know that he would soon be working for the enemy.

In June 1777, Wasmus joined British troops who were invading New York Colony. They had to cut down trees, cross rivers, and make trails. Thick brush slowed down the troops. Food for men and horses was limited. The delay gave the American **militia** time to gather more troops. The two sides finally met one another near Saratoga, New York.

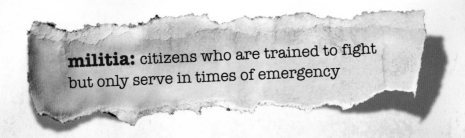

militia: citizens who are trained to fight but only serve in times of emergency

American militia attacked British soldiers during the Battle of Bennington.

THE BATTLE OF BENNINGTON

Before the two armies lined up at Saratoga, Wasmus and other troops were sent to gather supplies. After stealing horses, cattle, salt, and flour, they headed toward Bennington, Vermont. Then disaster struck.

American militia circled around them. Guns fired from the right and left. Wasmus chose a large oak tree for shelter. Behind the tree, he treated wounded men and watched as soldiers ran past in retreat.

When Wasmus stood up to leave, bullets whistled over his head. American fighters grabbed his arm and put a gun to his chest. They forced him to treat wounded American soldiers.

To Wasmus' surprise, the Americans weren't wearing uniforms like regular soldiers. Instead, they dressed in shirts, vests, and linen trousers. They didn't even wear stockings. He realized the British troops had been beaten by a bunch of patriot farmers.

Many men in American militias made their living by farming.

Because Wasmus was a doctor, he was treated better than most captured soldiers. Instead of being thrown in a prison, Wasmus spent the rest of the war in private American homes. He was fed well and treated kindly. But he did not speak English and could not communicate with his captors. Wasmus was restless, unhappy, and incredibly homesick. In 1783, he returned to Germany and continued his career as an army doctor.

A Turning Point in the War

Many British and German soldiers were killed at Bennington. As a result, the British army had fewer soldiers to fight in the Battle of Saratoga.

For a long time before the Battle of Saratoga, the British army seemed unstoppable. But local militia and the Continental army fought together for victory. The Americans began to realize they could win the war. The victory also encouraged France to send troops, ships, and supplies to help the American soldiers.

4 DAVID FANNING: LOYALIST ESCAPE ARTIST

a captured American

David Fanning glared at his captors. Fanning was a wealthy American farmer who remained loyal to Great Britain. He didn't like the idea of the colonists forming their own country. In May 1775, he organized other **Loyalists** to help fight the rebels.

Now three years later, Fanning was in prison for the tenth time. Earlier, Fanning had escaped by cutting ropes and jumping through windows. Sometimes he was released after promising to stop fighting. Once another Loyalist smuggled in two files and a knife. Fanning used them to cut through his cell's iron bars.

This time, his captors weren't taking any chances. They stripped him naked and chained him to the floor. But this wasn't enough to stop him. Fanning managed to wiggle out of his chains. Another prisoner gave him clothes, which he tied together to form a rope. He used the rope to escape through a window. He ran to safety as a guard fired at him.

In December 1778, Fanning was captured and chained again. After several days, he wiggled free from most of the chains. The guards gave up trying to keep him chained and instead kept irons around his ankles. For months Fanning lived in a small, cold room. Snow even fell in through the roof.

By February 1779, he was so thin he managed to slide off his iron chains. He loosened a window bar and used it to pry a board from the prison floor. Once he was downstairs, Fanning found a hole he had made during an earlier escape. By squeezing through the opening, he managed to escape again.

Loyalist: a colonist who was loyal to Great Britain during the Revolutionary War

a prisoner escaping through a window

FIGHTING THE REBELS

Fanning hid in the woods between escapes. He came out to lead raids. He and other Loyalists stole salt, weapons, and medicine from rebel camps. During one battle, Fanning was shot twice in the back. Soon after, the patriots offered him a pardon if he would just stay home. Fanning took the pardon, but he couldn't stay out of the fight forever. A year later, he was again attacking patriots.

The Continental army was now moving south. To avoid capture, Fanning led his men into North Carolina. There they continued their attacks. At one battle, Fanning was shot in his left arm. The bullet shattered a bone. Three weeks later, he was still very weak. But he planned to lead his men in a new attack on the rebels. His men helped lift him onto his horse. When the rebels fought back, Fanning's men scattered. He and the other Loyalists went into hiding.

By 1782, Fanning knew he was fighting a lost cause. He moved his family to Nova Scotia, an island near Canada. He remained loyal to Great Britain until his death.

American Loyalists fighting the patriots

5 JOSEPH MARTIN: AMERICAN PRIVATE

a young soldier marching

Fifteen-year-old Joseph Martin stared at the paper that would make him a soldier. He wanted to help punish the British for the way they treated Americans. He also wanted his country to be free. But was he really ready to join the army? His friend leaned over and pushed Martin's pen toward the paper. Martin sighed before signing his name. He dated the paper July 6, 1776.

For five years, Martin marched for miles, fighting in several battles. He suffered through a terrible winter at Valley Forge, Pennsylvania. The army provided weapons but very little food and other supplies. Despite his suffering, Martin still believed in the fight for liberty.

In 1781, Martin was stationed near Yorktown, Virginia. American and French soldiers surrounded the British. Martin was working through the night to build walls that would help protect the Americans.

Martin pulled his hat close to his face as rain fell. Suddenly a tall man appeared in the dark. Martin looked nervously toward his gun. Were the British coming?

Martin relaxed when the man disappeared into the night and returned with American officers. When the officers called the man "Your Excellency," Martin suddenly realized he was standing before General George Washington. Martin was shocked that Washington had come out here so close to the enemy. He could be shot!

A soldier at Valley Forge stands guard.

The next night Washington returned. He reached for a pickax and dug part of a trench. Martin would never forget how Washington worked alongside the troops at Yorktown.

In a few days, American and French troops were ready to fight. Soldiers raised an American flag as the signal to attack. Martin's heart swelled with pride at the sight. He grinned as the French shouted "Huzzah for the Americans!"

Martin and others were ordered to chop holes in the enemy's wooden fort. He charged across the dark field carrying an ax. By the light of grenades exploding in the sky, he found a weak spot in the British fort. He chopped his way through. Other soldiers charged in behind him. The Americans had captured the fort.

Fierce fighting continued for days. Martin was overwhelmed by the constant booming of guns and moaning of wounded soldiers. On October 19, 1781, the British finally surrendered. Martin watched as enemy soldiers marched away from the last major battle of the war.

The Battle at Yorktown was a major American victory.

At War in Winter

Colonists and British soldiers fought few battles during the winter. Instead they practiced marching and shooting. British soldiers settled around and in cities they controlled, such as New York and Philadelphia. Washington's troops spent difficult winters without proper supplies. Soldiers rarely had enough to eat.

Although many soldiers deserted during this time, Washington worked to keep his army together. His leadership throughout the war and afterward earned him the title "father of our country."

6 DEBORAH SAMSON: AN UNLIKELY SOLDIER

Most patriot women stayed home raising crops, caring for children, and making supplies for the troops. They fought off Loyalists who raided their homes. They also delivered messages and acted as spies. But a few women wanted to do more. They dressed as men and joined the fight against the British.

SOLDIER ROBERT SHURTLIFF

A tall soldier with a deep voice joined the Continental army in July 1782. The soldier was looking for adventure and wanted to help the colonists win the war. The soldier went by the name Robert Shurtliff. No one knew the soldier was really a woman named Deborah Samson.

Samson was careful not to make close friends with the other soldiers. She bathed apart from the men. The other soldiers thought she was just a shy boy.

Samson fought in several small battles and was wounded at the Battle of Tarrytown. Her fellow soldiers admired the young soldier who fought so bravely. Samson refused to see a doctor for her injuries. Instead she treated the wounds herself. It was the only way to keep her secret safe.

Women disguised themselves as men to fight.

23

Still known as Robert Shurtliff, Samson received an honorable discharge in 1783. After the war, Samson traveled and gave speeches about her adventures. The audience gasped as she marched on stage dressed as a soldier and demonstrated gun drills. Later she married and had children.

In 1804, famous patriot leader Paul Revere visited Samson. The government was beginning to give **pensions** to soldiers who had served in the war. Revere supported Samson's request for a pension. He wrote that though she was a woman, "she did a soldier's duty." With Revere's support, Samson received her pension.

pension: money paid to a person no longer serving in the army

Paul Revere

a woman firing a cannon at the Battle of Monmouth

Women at War

A few women went to war alongside their husbands. Many others worked in the camps doing laundry, cooking, nursing, and making soap. They also carried pitchers of water to men firing cannons. Water was needed to cool down the cannons after each firing. Sometimes these women even took over the firing of cannons when soldiers were wounded.

No one knows how many women helped out during the war. But one British officer declared that even if they destroyed all the American men, they'd still have to defeat the women.

7 THE WAR'S END

preparing the Treaty of Paris

In October 1781, the British surrendered at the Battle of Yorktown. It was the last major battle of the war. After the surrender, Washington moved his troops north into the Hudson Valley. British and American soldiers continued to fight small battles until the Treaty of Paris was signed in 1783.

Major fighting stopped after the British surrender at Yorktown.

When the British soldiers surrendered at Yorktown, their band played a song called "The World Turned Upside Down." The song showed just how surprised the soldiers were. They never thought the small, ill-equipped Continental army would beat them.

Many people who remained loyal to Britain moved to Canada or England. Their lands stood empty. Patriots moved into New York and Pennsylvania. Many in the south moved west to build large farms. New states formed, and the young nation grew.

Thousands of colonists took part in the fight for freedom. They fought against neighbors and friends. Many people were injured or killed. But the colonists had learned to work together. They created a new government and elected George Washington as the nation's first president. By 1787, they had written their own set of laws called the Constitution. This document still guides the country today.

The Constitution was signed on September 17, 1787.

GLOSSARY

colony (KAH-luh-nee)—a place that is settled by people from another country and is controlled by that country

discharge (DISS-charj)—an official leave from the army

Loyalist (LOI-uh-list)—a colonist who was loyal to Great Britain during the Revolutionary War

militia (muh-LISH-uh)—citizens who are trained to fight but only serve in times of emergency

pardon (PAHR-duhn)—to excuse a person from punishment

patriot (PAY-tree-uht)—an American colonist who disagreed with British rule of the American colonies

pension (PEN-shuhn)—money paid to a person no longer serving in the army

privateer (PRYE-vuh-teer)—a private ship that is authorized to attack enemy ships during wartime; the sailors aboard are also called privateers

rebel (REB-uhl)—a person who fights against a government

retreat (ri-TREET)—to move back or withdraw

BIBLIOGRAPHY

Fanning, David. *The Narrative of Colonel David Fanning.* Davidson, N.C.: Briarpatch Press, 1981.

Guba, Emil F. *Deborah Samson, Alias Robert Shurtliff, Revolutionary War Soldier.* Plymouth, Mass.: Jones River Press, 1994.

Martin, Joseph Plumb. *Yankee Doodle Boy: A Young Soldier's Adventures in the American Revolution.* New York: Holiday House, 1995.

Sherburne, Andrew. *Memoirs of Andrew Sherburne; A Pensioner of the Navy of the Revolution.* Freeport, N.Y.: Books for Libraries Press, 1970.

Wasmus, J. F. *An Eyewitness Account of the American Revolution and New England Life: The Journal of J.F. Wasmus, German Company Surgeon, 1776-1783.* New York: Greenwood Press, 1990.

Young, Alfred F. *Masquerade: The Life and Times of Deborah Sampson, Continental Soldier.* New York: Alfred A. Knopf, 2004.

READ MORE

Beller, Susan Provost. *Yankee Doodle and the Redcoats: Soldiering in the Revolutionary War.* Soldiers on the Battlefront. Minneapolis: Twenty-First Century Books, 2008.

Micklos, John, Jr. *The Brave Women and Children of the American Revolution.* The Revolutionary War Library. Berkley Heights, N.J.: Enslow Publishers, 2009.

Raum, Elizabeth. *The Revolutionary War: An Interactive History Adventure.* You Choose. Mankato, Minn.: Capstone Press, 2010.

INTERNET SITES

FactHound offers a safe, fun way to find Internet sites related to this book. All of the sites on FactHound have been researched by our staff.

Here's all you do:

Visit *www.facthound.com*

Type in this code: 9781429647397

INDEX